COMPACT DISC PAGE AND BAND INFORMATION

Music Minus One

3715

3

Beethoven: 'Cello Sonata in A, Opus 69

Music Minus One • 50 Executive Boulevard • Elmsford, New York 10523-1325
Website: www.musicminusone.com   Phone: 914-592-1188 • Fax: 914-592-3575

Beethoven
Sonata in A major, Opus 69
for 'cello and piano

Allegro ma non tanto

3715

Scherzo

Allegro molto

8

3715

3715
III

3715

Duo in B Flat Major

G. Telemann
ed. S. Thomas

Affettuoso

Allegro

3715

18

3715

Andante

Molto Allegro

3715

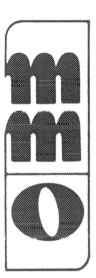

Beethoven
'Cello Sonata in A, Opus 69

G.P.Telemann
'Cello Duet in Bb

3715